AF824685

Parents' Guide To Better Borrowing

Joy Alford-Brand, JD

Copyright © 2019 Joy Alford-Brand, JD

All rights reserved.

ISBN: 978-0-9978246-1-2

CONTENTS

	Introduction	ii
1	Before College	1
2	The Award Letter	2
3	Calculating Net Price	5
4	Lather, Rinse, Repeat!	6
5	Types of Loans	7
6	Tips & Strategies	12
7	Understanding Interest	29
8	Servicer Handbook	37

INTRODUCTION

Congratulations on your child's completion of High School! What a wonderful achievement and the first major milestone in life. While you are celebrating your child's commencement, I'm sure you have already been thinking about the next chapter, the college or university your student will attend. It is such an exciting time for you and your family! After you've served the last piece of cake and sent the last thank you card, it's time to get down to the business of figuring out how to pay for the next four years.

If you are lucky, you (or someone else), has put aside funds for your student's college tuition and expenses. If you are like most families, you may be wondering how to find the money to pay for your student's college education. By purchasing this guide, you've taken the first step in paying for college in the most painless, cheapest way.

Let's go over a few facts that will show you why I'm becoming concerned enough about student loan debt to write this guide. First of all, on a national level we have $1.5 - $1.6 trillion dollars in student loan debt spread over approximately forty-four million borrowers. Nearly half of student loans (43% to be exact), are not being paid. Either they are in default, deferment or forbearance. The scariest statistics show that the fastest growing demographic of student loan borrowers are actually the parents of students and senior citizens. The average amount of debt that demographic is taking out on behalf of their students is $15,000 - $16,000. The total amount of student loan debt people over the age of sixty have accumulated is $85.4 billion and that figure is growing. This means that more and more people are taking on student loan debt as they get older and failing to pay it off. I think we can do a better job of borrowing if we are given the right facts and information.

Now, let's get down to business and give you the information you need to borrow better and avoid the pitfalls of student loan debt.

CHAPTER 1 - BEFORE COLLEGE

The FAFSA

This guide assumes your student has already applied to schools and filled out the Free Application for Federal Student Aid (FAFSA). If you haven't done that yet, and you are within the timeframe for submitting it, head on over to the studentaid.gov website and follow the links to fill out the FAFSA form. You cannot get access to federal student financial aid without filling it out. Check your state's deadlines from the list on the studentaid.gov website to make sure you are submitting the form in a timely manner. If you need assistance filling out the FAFSA, you can use the help tool on the studentaid.gov website or check with the college student aid office for FAFSA application resources.

While you fill out your FAFSA form and submit it to the federal student aid website, the school your student attends ultimately issues the student's award letter and disburses the federal funds. This is why we are going to start with the award letter the school sends out after the federal government issues it's Student Aid Report (SAR).

Tips:

- Your student will need a Federal Student Aid ID to fill out the FAFSA. Make sure your student keeps that information in a safe place because they will need it all the way through college and beyond graduation to manage their student loans.
- You'll generally fill out the FAFSA around the same time your student is applying to colleges. You can list up to ten on the FAFSA form.
- Make sure your student is involved in filling out the FAFSA. They need to be aware of the process from start to finish, including the loans they are getting and the terms for each loan.

CHAPTER 2 - THE AWARD LETTER

The financial aid award letter you receive from the school is an important tool in determining where your student can afford to attend and how to pay for it. Hopefully, you've been looking at the net price and net costs of the schools your student is considering applying to. Cost should definitely be a factor you and your student are considering when applying to colleges.

Each college sends out a unique financial aid award letter. There is no standardized letter or format that every college has to adhere to. This can make things very confusing when you are looking at the net price and net cost of college.

First, you need to be aware of the true cost of attending each school. While award letters generally list the basic expenses like tuition and fees, they may not include room and board, books and supplies, let alone living expenses such as parking, insurance, cell phone expenses and other living expenses. Ideally, you have researched these additional expenses so you can adjust the amounts in each award letter accordingly. Check with the schools your student has applied to and see if they have a budget breakdown they can provide to you to help you figure out the sticker price. Remember, their budget may not include every expense your student may have to pay to attend that school.

Second, you need to read the financial aid letter carefully. Make sure you understand each item under the financial aid package that the school is offering. Sometimes it's hard to tell if what you are being offered is a loan or a gift. Make sure you are very clear about each item in your financial aid package before you accept it since award letters generally do not contain the terms of each item contained in your award package. It is your responsibility to know what you are accepting and agreeing to.

Items listed in your financial aid package typically can include the following:

Federal Loans/Students: These are loans provided by the federal government. They generally have a lower interest rate than private loans and may include repayment assistance and/or forgiveness. They are either subsidized or unsubsidized.

Federal Loans/Parent PLUS: Again, these are loans provided by the federal government. They generally have a lower interest rate than private loans and may include repayment assistance and/or forgiveness. There are important differences between loans for students and loans for parents that we will cover. This guide will cover them in section V.

Grants: This is considered gifted aid. Federal grants typically do not have to be paid back as long as you comply with the terms thereof (note the TEACH grant has had recent issues with conversions to loans based on students failing to comply with the terms).

Scholarships: This is considered gifted aid. Money from any one of a number of sources designed to pay all or a portion of a student's education expenses. Scholarships do not have to be paid back.

Federal Work-Study: You have to qualify to receive a work-study placement by demonstrating financial need.

State Financial Aid: You may qualify for additional financial aid from your state. While you may have to apply for this separately from the FAFSA, your school may include it on your award letter. Make sure you check with your state to see if you qualify for any financial assistance.

Cost of Attendance (COA): This is the sticker price for attending a college or university. If the school is calculating it, the COA probably will not include every expense, just direct expenses like tuition and fees.

Expected Family Contribution (EFC): When you fill out your FAFSA form, the Department of Education will calculate your EFC. This is the amount that your family will be expected to pay toward your COA.

Demonstrated Financial Need: After you complete the FAFSA, the Department of Education will send a report to the school's financial aid office that will include your EFC. The school will then calculate your financial need and award your need-based financial aid, this is generally based on your EFC and includes all gifted aid and subsidized loans. If your need-based aid is not enough to cover the COA, the school will then award you aid that is not need-based, this will include unsubsidized loans. Finally, if your gifted aid, subsidized loans and unsubsidized loans are not enough to cover the COA, your school will offer Parent PLUS loans.

If you don't completely understand every part of your award letter, call the school's financial aid office and ask them to explain it. You may have to make an appointment and discuss it in person. Either way, do not sign on the dotted line until you fully understand the complete financial aid package.

CHAPTER 3 - CALCULATING NET PRICE

Now that you know what your financial aid package contains, you can start to weigh how much each college will cost. Again, this needs to be a critical part of the decision making process when choosing a college. If you aren't careful when determining these numbers, your student (and you, the parent), could wind up significantly under water on your college education expenses.

Net Price: This number is determined by subtracting your grants, scholarships and work-study amounts from your total COA. Do not take for granted the net price calculated on your award letter as the correct net price. It may not include many of the hidden or indirect expenses you need to factor in to get your true total COA.

Let's start by calculating the net price of your student's college education. You calculate this figure by first calculating the total COA. This means you add in all indirect expenses like a computer, parking/insurance, room and board and books and supplies. Once you've added all indirect expenses to the direct expenses, like tuition and fees, you'll know your true total COA. It won't hurt to check out school websites for their college net price calculators. While they are not all inclusive, they can help you get an idea of the cost of living expenses while attending school there. At this point, calculate your net price for each school you are considering. I suggest using a spreadsheet to keep track of your direct, indirect, financial aid awards, and net price calculations for each school. That will make it easier to compare and determine which school has the best net price. I created a spreadsheet specifically for this purpose that you can download at newcashview.com/resources/student-loan-resources/ for your convenience.

CHAPTER 4 - LATHER, RINSE REPEAT!

Remember, you'll have to fill out a FAFSA and go through the award letter process for each year your student is in school! Be vigilant about this task because prices and values can change dramatically from one year to the next.

CHAPTER 5 - TYPES OF LOANS

While it would be wonderful to have your education completely paid for by grants and scholarships, that is not likely to happen. For the most part, your student will probably be funding their college education with loans. It's wonderful that we have access to student loans that we can use to help us pay for college, but there quite a few things you should know before you choose to sign on the dotted line.

A. Private vs. Federal

While there are circumstances when a private student loan may be beneficial, your best bet is to always opt for federal student loans if you can. In a nutshell, they have better interest rates and most of them have repayment assistance or forgiveness, if you find you can't pay them at some point. Private loans generally do not. For that reason, we are going to stick to federal loans in this guide. If you have to go the private loan route, make sure you understand all the terms and get the lowest interest rate possible.

1. Federal Loan Types (taken from the U.S. Department of Education website):

a. Direct Unsubsidized

Program details (as of August 2019)

- For undergraduate students; financial need is not required.
- You are fully responsible for interest which begins to accrue on disbursement.
- For loans first disbursed on or after July 1, 2019, and before July 1, 2020: 4.53% interest rate for loans made to undergraduate students.

- **NOTE: You're responsible for interest during all periods**

- Max annual award allowed for first year undergraduate students:

$5,500 to $9,500 (less any subsidized amounts received for same period) depending on grade level and dependency status.

For total lifetime limit, go to https://studentaid.ed.gov/sa/types/loans/subsidized-unsubsidized

b. **Direct Subsidized**

Program details (as of August 2019)

- For undergraduate students (only) who have financial need .

- For loans first disbursed on or after July 1, 2019, and before July 1, 2020, interest rate is 4.53%.

- **NOTE: You're not usually charged interest on the loan during certain periods, such as when you're in school at least half-time.**

- Max annual award allowed for first year undergraduate students:

Up to $5,500 to $9,500 depending on grade level and dependency status.

For total lifetime limit, go to https://studentaid.ed.gov/sa/types/loans/subsidized-unsubsidized

c. Direct PLUS

Program details (as of August 2019)

- For parents who are borrowing money to pay for their dependent undergraduate child's education.
- For loans first disbursed on or after July 1, 2019, and before July 1, 2020, interest rate is 7.08%.
- FINANCIAL NEED IS NOT REQUIRED
- Borrower must not have adverse credit.
- Interest begins to accrue upon disbursement, and you are responsible for payments right away.
- Max annual award allowed: **NONE**

Maximum amount is cost of attendance minus any other financial aid student receives:

NOT ELIGIBLE FOR INCOME DRIVEN REPAYMENT!!! INCOME CONTINGENT REPAYMENT ONLY!

https://studentaid.ed.gov/sa/sites/default/files/federal-loan-programs.pdf

d. Direct Consolidation

Yes, you can consolidate your loans when you/your student is still in school, but I do not advise it, you could lose your six month repayment grace period. I'll address consolidation in section VI.

Obviously, the best loan to get is the subsidized loan. It saves your student money in the long run by not accruing interest while your student is enrolled at least half-time in school. As you can see, unsubsidized loans begin accruing interest as soon as they are disbursed, adding a substantial amount to the balance of the loan your student will be responsible for after graduation.

The least favorable loans, in my opinion, are Parent PLUS loans. Here are a few reasons why:

- Schools will include Parent PLUS loans on their award letters, but typically these loans are not part of your student's financial aid package. Instead, they are included on the award letter as an item under the financial aid package to cover any shortfall in the financial aid that is awarded directly to the student. In fact, as long as your credit is good, parents can qualify for an unlimited amount of Parent PLUS loans in order to pay for your student's college education.

- Parents have to apply separately for PLUS loans and the interest rate is two points higher than either type of loan available to your student.

- Additionally, you should know that if you take out PLUS loans but are unable to repay them, you could, in fact, treasury offset on your future tax returns and/or a partial garnishment of your future social security payment.

- While you can consolidate Parent PLUS loans or ask for deferment or forbearance, Parent PLUS loans are not eligible for any Income Driven Repayment plan. This means the only repayment plans available to parents are the 10 year standard repayment plan or the Income Contingent Repayment plan (ICR).

The basic terms of the ICR plan are a payment based on 20% of your discretionary income for 25 years. During the ICR plan, interest will accrue until the outstanding principal amount (original amount when loan entered repayment), is 10% greater than the original principal amount. After that, interest continues to accrue but is not capitalized.

CHAPTER 6 - TIPS & STRATEGIES

Parents, this section combines information for every type of federal student loan, for both types of borrowers (you and your student). Please note: student loan debt is complicated. While you should read and become familiar with this entire guide, make sure you get to know your student's financial aid office and be persistent about getting your questions answered before you sign on the dotted line.

You generally cannot double dip/overlap forgiveness plans/programs. If your state offers a forgiveness program and you only have federal loans, you can only use the state program or the federal program that fits your circumstances. You cannot enroll in both programs simultaneously.

Make the servicer handbook your bible, keep track of everything. I've included it after the Tips and Strategies section.

Here are some tips and strategies you and your students should consider to keep your college costs under control.

A. BEFORE COLLEGE

1. Stick to in-state schools. Consider picking a school based on a cost-benefit analysis. While I totally get that we want our students to go to the school that is the best at their chosen field of study, not everyone has to go to NYU to get a business degree. Living in NYC is really, really expensive. A better choice might be a local in-state university where the cost of living might be much cheaper. Strongly consider the location of the school when you are pricing out colleges.

2. Start off at a local community college or pursue concurrent enrollment, if at all possible. Consider starting out at community college. Get your associate's degree first and then go to a University to complete your bachelor's degree. Local community colleges are much cheaper than most four year universities, public or private, in state or out of state. The collegeboard.org website says it all, (constant dollar tuition

and fees for two year public college is $3,810 in 17/18 as compared to four year public school average of $9,270).

Of course, this may not be practical for everyone, especially if you have your heart set on getting a specialized degree that is only offered out of state or in a remote location. Being flexible in how you approach your college education can save you big, BIG bucks later on. The other argument I get about this is "not all the credits will transfer." Make sure you do your homework first. Some states offer things like in-state tuition caps for community colleges and also a credit transfer program to four year schools in the same university system.

Many people disagree with this course of action because the attrition rate (meaning the number of people who don't finish community college), is pretty high. The truth is, not everyone finishes their bachelor's degree, either. If you don't complete the program, at least the amount of debt you will end up with will be less than if you dropped out from a four-year school. Also, I think this shows the skewed thinking about student loan debt. If you compare your savings at a two year school with the cost of the first two years at an in-state, public university, the sheer amount of money you'll save should be motivation to complete the program. Oh, and you'll also have an associate's degree when you're done!

Also, consider a vocational school, trade school or an apprenticeship. We need people to build things, repair things and generally keep our infrastructure maintained. I believe college isn't right for everyone and it shouldn't be. If we don't have anyone to build, repair and maintain our infrastructures, they will eventually stop working and that is not a good thing at all. Maybe your student enjoys building or working with their hands. If so, a career in the trades could be the path to a happy and wealthy life.

3. Live at home. Most parents I say this to bristle at this suggestion. Some get downright mad at it, but I stand by this advice. Parents want their kid to "mature" or "figure out who they are." Well, the truth is, that's going to happen no matter

what and college may or may not help them mature (everyone knows someone who racked up big student loans right before getting kicked out of school for partying too much). Your kid can either save a ton of money by living at home while they are going to college, or they can live at home for the foreseeable future while they try to find a job in their field that pays enough for them to make their big student loan payment and move out.

Again, check out school websites for college net price calculators. While they are not all inclusive, they can help you get an idea of the cost of living expenses while attending school there. Remember, it's generally much cheaper to live at home!

If you can't live at home, don't rule out living on campus. It may be cheaper, depending on the circumstances. You can also check out sites like zillow.com to see how much it costs to live off campus in terms of rent. Also talk with other students at the school to see what the consensus is on living expense affordability. Usually, when you are touring colleges, you have the chance to ask questions and most people will be happy to chat you up about their school.

One of the smartest things I did was choose schools I could commute to. That meant two things: first, I picked in state, public universities (read as: they are much cheaper options with excellent degree programs in my chosen field of study). Second, out of the seven years I was in college and law school, I only lived on campus for one year. As a result, I was able to take out the smallest amount of loan money possible which eased my burden after graduation (in case I had trouble finding a JOB after graduation).

4. Get a job. I've had so many parents tell me "I don't want my kids to work while they're in school. Their job is going to school." While there may be circumstances that justify keeping your student from working while in college, I think the average college student should be working at the very least in the summer. I worked two or sometimes three jobs

when I was in school (as an undergraduate and at least one job in my second and third years of law school, we weren't allowed to work during our first year of law school), and not only did it allow me to eat, keep my car insured and gas in the tank, it also taught me important lessons about time management, responsibility, and having skin in the game. I realize times are different and every situation is different but, the goal is to graduate with as little debt as possible. Also, working during college is a good way to ease into "adulting" by learning things like what a W-2 is for, time management, how to work with others and so on.

5. CAREFULLY consider joining the military/GI bill. Do your research thoroughly before signing on the dotted line. If the military seems right for you, it could be a great way for you to get real world experience and pay for college. Just know that there are definite pros and cons including winding up doing a different job in a completely different place than you asked for. Being a GI means the government gets to tell you what to do. If that doesn't sound like it's for you, by all means, choose a different path.

6. Make sure college is right for your child! Ask your child if they are going to college because they think they are supposed to, or so they can get a job, OR are they going to study something they love and are passionate about? I realize this will not be popular with every parent out there who is reading this, but I hope you know I'm saying it out of love.... When you say "I want my kid to have the college experience," consider asking your child if they feel college is right for him or her.

   Kids who go off to college without money in the bank to pay for it do not understand that they are taking on debt that he or she (or even you) may not be able to pay off if he or she cannot find a job after graduation. Also, don't forget that student loan debt is generally not dischargeable in bankruptcy and the borrower's tax refund can be offset, and their social security payments can be garnished. Please don't come after me with clubs and pitchforks, I just want the best for you and your child!

You have to look at college not as a rite of passage but as an investment. This includes picking a degree/course of study that provides verifiable employment after graduation, this is your ROI (return on investment). Hopefully, your student's degree and passion are in alignment.

7. Only take out the minimal amount of student loan debt needed in order for your student to complete the school year or that they can reasonably expect to pay back after college. A good rule of thumb is to keep your student loan debt at or below your first year's salary. So, if your industry pays a starting salary of $35,000 a year, try to keep your total student loan debt under $35,000.

   Also, remember, student loan debt proceeds are intended to cover educational expenses. This includes tuition, books, and reasonable living expenses while you are enrolled in school. It does not include luxury items like entertainment (video games, expensive concert tickets, extravagant eating out), personal care (getting your nails done, expensive hairdos, high end hand bags or clothes/shoes or sporting equipment), or spring break trips. If you have money left over after you graduate, you should use it to pay down your accrued interest.

   We really need to help educate our young people about the consequences of their actions. We need to guide them in understanding the true value of a college education and how to maximize the return on their investment because truly, a college education is an investment in the student and their future. We want to make sure we help them understand it can be a bad investment if it isn't managed correctly, so let's try to help them see how to make choices that will make it a good or even great investment!

   Again, for parents, it's very, very important to make sure the student is completely involved in every step of the student loan process. They should, at the very least, help fill out the FAFSA form or fill it out themselves. Make sure they are involved with every decision about what student loans they are taking out, even the parent PLUS loans, and how much is being spent on their education.

I'm not suggesting abandoning your child or letting them sink or swim. What I'm saying is, sit down with them and involve them in the process. Teach them to do the work while you are standing by as a safety net. This is a great opportunity to let them learn some "adulting" skills while you are there to help if they make a mistake. This also has the benefit of giving them ownership in their financial situation. If they see how much things cost and what they will have to pay back at some point, they'll be more likely to take their studies seriously, graduate, and be successful in paying off their debt.

8. Look for local scholarships. Just remember to weigh the effort of applying for the scholarship against the amount of money you'll receive. While every little bit helps, there is a point of diminishing returns.

9. Protect your future. I've already talked about this but I'm going to say it again. Parents, this piece of advice is really directed at you. If you have unpaid federal student loan debt, the government can garnish your Social Security payment when it comes time for you to start receiving Social Security. The U.S. Treasury can also do something called a "treasury offset" of your tax refund to pay on your student loan debt. This is true whether you took the loans out for yourself or for your student. If you are a guarantor of the loans, meaning you signed on the dotted line, you are responsible for repaying them. Period. Also, remember that student loan debt is generally not dischargeable in bankruptcy (this cannot be repeated too many times).

   This also means you should put your mask on first. You know when you are in a plane listening to the flight attendant's safety talk before the plane takes off? Remember the part of that talk where they tell you to put your mask on first then help the person next to you put their mask on? This idea applies to paying for your kid's college, too. If you are thinking of dipping into your 401(k), or other retirement fund, to pay for your kid to go to college, I strongly urge you to reconsider. Your child has time on their side so they are better able to pay down their debt and invest (meaning take advantage of time and compounding).

Now, hear me out. If you raid your retirement fun, you lose the advantage of time and compounding. This potentially puts you in a financially precarious position at a time when you may not be able to work, resulting in your children having to assist you financially. The hard truth is, if you're lucky enough to have a retirement account, you probably can't replace the earnings once you've taken money out of that account. Consider your options if you don't have the funds you need to survive on when it's time for you to retire and think twice before raiding your retirement fund for your kid's college tuition. Do your kids a favor and stabilize your own finances, then you can help your kids with theirs. Remember, don't shoot the messenger, I'm saying this with love!

Finally, if you go against this advice and raid your retirement account, you won't be the first or the last parent to go that route. I certainly won't think any less of you and I respect your decision as a parent. Just make sure you've exhausted every other option first.

B. IN COLLEGE

1. While your student is still in school, encourage them to pay on their accruing interest, if all possible.

2. If you are planning to consolidate, don’t do it if you are in your grace period, it will cut it short. I’ve said this before, but it bears repeating. If you can’t make payments after your grace period ends, contact your servicer and apply for an IDR, if appropriate.

3. Start keeping track of your loans as soon as possible and pay attention to which ones are subsidized and which ones aren’t.

Make the Student Loan Servicer Handbook in the next section your bible!

4. Follow all the steps the Department of Education (DOE) requires (including student loan checklist, exit counseling, etc.).

5. GRADUATE. While it is true that a college degree doesn't guarantee you a job, don't take out loans and then drop out. The fact is, borrowers who don't finish school are less likely to have the income needed to pay off their student loans. There are plenty of statistics that support this statement. If you would like to learn more about them, you can check out the National Center for Education Studies Fast Facts website: https://nces.ed.gov/fastfacts/display.asp?id=900

C. AFTER COLLEGE

1. Parents, be aware that your Parent PLUS loans will be defaulted into the 10 year standard repayment plan. If you can afford the payment, I would suggest staying in that plan. If you can't afford the payment, you need to know that Parent PLUS loans are only eligible for the Income Contingent Repayment plan and you have to consolidate your loans first. Choosing to apply for this repayment plan means you need to understand how the Income Contingent Repayment plan works. We've covered this before but, here's a recap: you'll pay more in interest because the repayment plan lasts 25 years but your monthly payment will be capped at 20% of your discretionary income (determined by a Department of Education formula based on your household size). After 25 years, you'll be eligible for forgiveness.

   Another way to say this is your student has more repayment options than you do. This is why I advise parents not to take out Parent PLUS loans if they can help it. You can always help your student make their loan payment after graduation.

2. Use the student loan payment estimator to figure out what you think your payment will be and whether you would benefit from an IDR. You can find the payment estimator

here:
https://studentloans.gov/myDirectLoan/repaymentEstimator.action

3. Make a plan. Have your student fill out the student loan information spreadsheet or form. Make sure they do NOT lose track of your loans. You could have quite a few and every one MUST be paid on time. With 12 to 20 loans, it may be easy to forget to pay one. Be diligent about this. One missed payment could spell an interest rate disaster. List out your interest rates, monthly payments, and type of loan for each loan.

   Determine if you might qualify for Public Service Loan Forgiveness (PSLF). (Understand the difference between Teacher Loan Forgiveness (TLF) and PSLF—if you qualify for PSLF, and you have enough debt that would make it worthwhile, apply for that rather than TLF. TLF is useful if you only have a small amount of debt. TLF and PSLF are consecutive/sequential).

   a. Apply for an Income Driven Repayment (IDR) Plan - Pay attention to the interest benefits/rules for each IDR plan. Be careful when changing IDR plans. Make sure you know the rules about capitalization of interest, etc. before you do. Remember, you can stay in an IDR even if your income is too high for a reduced monthly payment (however, staying in the plan can extend the length of time you make payments before you make enough to qualify for forgiveness and you may have paid the loan off by then). As long as you have eligible loans, you do not have to consolidate to apply for an IDR. Remember, Parent PLUS loans are only eligible for the Income Driven Repayment plan.

   b. Stick to your plan - Make sure you are not missing any deadlines for recertification of income, family size or employment (for TLF or PSLF). (PARENTS - this is true for the ICR plan payment, too!) Make sure you are notifying your servicer when you change your information (name, address, email or telephone). If you fail to update your contact information with your servicer, you may miss important information which could cause delays and missed/late payments.

c. Choose a repayment method - Avalanche vs. IDR. This is appropriate if you are not in an IDR or qualifying for PSLF. If you start down this road, request that your servicer NOT ADVANCE YOUR PAYMENT DATE if possible. If you start taking advantage of your servicer advancing your payment due date and skipping payments, your interest will continue to accrue and this could do more harm than good. Do your best to keep making your monthly payment. If you decide not to consolidate your loans and decide to pay extra on a loan while making minimum payments on the others, use the avalanche method. Pay off the loan with the highest interest rate first (avoid the snowball method, do not accelerate payment on the wrong loan). We'll talk more about servicers advancing payments in the Servicer Handbook section.

d. Consider staying in the 10 year standard repayment plan. All student loans are defaulted into the 10 year standard repayment plan. If you can manage it, try to stay in that plan rather than switching to an income based repayment plan. The payments will be higher but, you'll be in the plan for 10 years as opposed to 20 years or more. AND you'll wind up saving in interest, therefore paying less for your student loans over time.

4. Carefully weigh consolidation - it may be the only way to resolve a defaulted loan or (if you are a parent borrower, it may be the only way to get you into the ICR plan). Remember, you can generally only rehabilitate or consolidate loans once. After consolidating your interest rate will be an average of the interest rates on all your consolidated loans. If

you have already consolidated your loans, you can't consolidate again, unless you have new loans.

a. Consider NOT consolidating and employ the avalanche debt repayment system instead. Maintain your minimum monthly payments on your other loans, then choose the loan with the highest interest rate and pay it off as quickly as possible. This may mean paying off your unsubsidized loans before your subsidized loans, each situation is unique.

b. You should never have to pay a fee to consolidate your loans or apply for repayment plans.

5. Carefully weigh refinancing with a private lender. BEWARE! YOU WILL LOSE FORGIVENESS & REDUCED INTEREST BENEFITS OF IDRs. (LOOK AT RULES OF THUMB FOR REFI.)

   a. Consolidation

      - I refer to consolidation as applicable to federal student loans.

      - If you want to apply for a student loan forgiveness program, you'll have to consolidate if you have federal student loans that don't qualify.

      - For federal loans only! Private loans will never qualify for any kind of federal consolidation loan or forgiveness programs.

      - Gives you a single payment with a fixed interest rate based on the average of the interest rates on all the loans being consolidated.

      - Completing the application is FREE. Don't be duped into paying for it. You can complete the application on the studentloan.gov website.

- Consolidating may be a smart choice if you are in default since it is essentially putting you in a new loan that will then be current. No matter what, consider every factor before consolidating.

- If you can't make your payments and you haven't consolidated your loans, you can always ask to defer ONLY your subsidized loans (since they don't accrue interest during the 6 month term of a hardship deferment), and continue paying on your unsubsidized loans.

- BEWARE!

- If you consolidate your unsubsidized AND subsidized loans, you'll be consolidating them into a whole new loan and you'll likely lose any interest discount or benefit. You could choose to consolidate ONLY your unsubsidized loans and leave your subsidized loans as is.

- If you are interested in consolidating your loans (for example, if you want to apply for PSLF which only takes certain federal loans as we mentioned before), you need to know a few things.

- When you consolidate, you lose any qualifying payments you've already made towards forgiveness. For example, if you are five years into making payments, you'll have to start over if you consolidate. So, if you are consolidating your federal loans because some of them are not eligible for PSLF and you want to convert them into eligible loans, consider carefully how many payments you've made and whether or not it's worth it for you to lose qualifying payments to qualify under PSLF.

- It's ideal to consolidate earlier in the life of your loan. However, if you consolidate during your grace period (as your loan is entering repayment), you could lose the remainder of your grace period, meaning you'll have to start making payments right away.

- If you consolidate your unsubsidized AND subsidized loans, you'll be consolidating them into a whole new loan and you'll likely lose any interest discount or benefit. You could choose to consolidate ONLY your unsubsidized loans and leave your subsidized loans as is.

- You can only consolidate once (except in limited circumstances).

- Consolidating always extends the length of your loan. Just like refinancing your mortgage. This means you will end up paying a lot more in interest over the life of the loan. The flip side of this is it will often lower your payment. Again, just like refinancing your mortgage.

b. Refinancing

- I refer to refinancing as the method of using private loans to refinance or consolidate your federal student loans.

- I DO NOT ADVOCATE REFINANCING YOUR FEDERAL LOANS USING PRIVATE LOANS EXCEPT IN VERY SLIM CIRCUMSTANCES. ONCE YOU LOSE YOUR FEDERAL LOAN STATUS, YOU CAN NEVER GET IT BACK!

- Having said that, here are my rules of thumb for loans that do not qualify for any forgiveness program like private consolidation/refinancing loans:

- You'll get a better FIXED interest rate. (Beware of the variable interest rate loan!) This is a no brainer. The interest rate you pay is basically the cost of borrowing the money. The cheaper you can get it, the better. This is my most important rule when consolidating.

- You'll get a substantially lower payment. Monthly cash flow is usually our most immediate issue, in general. Whatever consolidation loan you choose, it ideally should provide you with a substantially lower payment.

- The length of your loan will not be substantially extended. Of course there will be some extension, that's the nature of the beast, but check carefully to make sure you're not agreeing to an unconscionable repayment term.

- No penalty for early repayment. This is another big one. I've heard of some consolidation loans penalizing borrowers for early repayment. Ask if this is a term of the loan. If it is, run away!

- No co-signer. Attention parents of adult children, do everything you can to avoid co-signing for your adult child's student loan. Or any loan for anyone, for that matter. If the consolidation loan will require a co-signer, I would avoid it unless you are already a co-signer on the loans to be consolidated and you'll be getting better overall terms by consolidating. Remember, don't co-sign a loan unless you are willing to pay it back.

6. AVOID FORBEARANCE. If at all possible, avoid forbearance because interest accrues during periods of forbearance and then it can be capitalized. This is true whether your federal loans are subsidized or unsubsidized.

7. AVOID DEFAULT. Do not make a payment late, you will be placed in delinquent status and technically, you are in default. Remember, you can't be in default and apply for an IDR or maintain a reduced monthly payment. If you default, your loan can also be accelerated. If you can't make your payment, notify your servicer immediately. DO NOT WAIT! A forbearance is much better than default. Remember, you can only rehabilitate defaulted loans once.

8. Remember, student loans must be paid back unless you die or you are either disabled or a disabled veteran. This means that you shouldn't take them out if you aren't willing to pay them back. This is true for students AND their parents who either take out their own loans for the students or co-sign loans for their student (see 5b above). I've filed bankruptcies for parents of adult children who were paying student loan debt for their kids and they couldn't afford to pay the loans and their living expenses. Don't rely on your kids to pay off the loans you take out for them. Many of them are having enough trouble paying their own student loans, let alone the loans their parents took out on their behalf.

   Finally, remember what I said earlier. If you go against this advice and take out or co-sign loans for your student, you won't be the first or the last parent to go that route. I certainly won't think any less of you and I respect your decision as a parent. Again, just make sure you've exhausted every other option first.

C. Rehabilitation -

For this section, please see the text from the rehabilitation page from the Consumer Financial Protection Bureau website reprinted below:

https://www.consumerfinance.gov/paying-for-college/repay-student-debt/#federal:yes:yes:no

Your debt collector is required by law to offer you this income-driven rehabilitation payment plan.

> If a debt collector refuses to offer you an option for which you believe you qualify, submit a complaint online or by calling (855) 411-2372. Rehabilitation won't repair your credit completely—your previous missed payments may still show up on your credit report—but any default notation will be removed. Your servicer or debt collector may ask you to provide documentation to demonstrate that you need a lower payment than they are suggesting. When negotiating with your debt collector, the law requires your collector to determine your payment amount based on your income; however, once you agree to a payment plan, you are required to make your monthly payment in order to rehabilitate your defaulted loan.
>
> Contact your servicer or debt collector immediately to learn more about your options and to make arrangements to bring your loan out of default.
>
> Ask the debt collector for specific information about fees. The costs associated with bringing your loan out of default may vary substantially depending on your individual circumstances.

When speaking with your servicer or a debt collector, be sure that you have written documentation about what federal student debt you owe. If you are concerned that you never borrowed certain loans, check the National Student Loan Data System. If the loan does not appear there, contact the collector and inform the collector of the problem. Remember, that system shows only your federal student loans, not your private student loans.

9. If your loan is placed with a collection agency, learn your rights. The Fair Debt Collections Practices Act rules apply. Be advised you will be charged collection fees (an amount calculated based on the total balance due on the loan).

10. Decide whether to enroll in autopay for your monthly student loan payment. Pros: you can save on your interest rate (usually .25 or .50 a point in interest rate savings). Cons: If something goes wrong with your payment and it gets bumped to a higher amount, you could be surprised by the adjusted autodraft. It can save you money if you sign up for it, just make sure you are paying attention to your payment.

11. If you are making more than your minimum monthly payment, make sure you are notifying your servicer about applying the excess payment correctly. Make sure your payment is applied correctly.

    - There is no penalty for early repayment, however the rule is anything you pay must be applied to interest and fees before principal. If you pay more than your monthly payment, the excess is applied to future payments unless you notify the servicer that you do not want your date advanced.

12. Make sure you understand the tax consequences of married filing jointly versus married filing separately when it comes to using your adjusted gross income (AGI) for IDR or ICR repayment plan purposes. You should also ask your accountant about the tax consequences of forgiven, discharged, or cancelled debt.

13. Don't forget to take advantage of your student loan interest tax deduction!

14. Check to see if your state has any forgiveness programs available.

15. Make a budget and stick to it. Include saving for retirement as part of your budget. While some would argue that you shouldn't be saving for retirement when you still have debt, treat it like your student loans. Put your monthly retirement savings amount on a sliding scale. One way to do it is transfer the money you were paying toward your student loans to retirement savings as you pay your loans off (of course, this doesn't work if you have a single consolidation loan but, you get the point).

16. Remember, the longer you have the debt the more expensive (interest) it will be. There is no penalty for early repayment so you should be working toward that goal.

17. Understand income to payment ratio! The more you earn, the higher your payment will be in any plan other than the 10 year standard repayment plan. This also means think about how getting married will impact your student loan payment. Most IDR plans require you to factor in your spouse's income when calculating your payment.

18. Keep an eye on your credit report! You should be monitoring your credit REPORT (not necessarily your credit score), by running your free reports annually. I call it The Four Month Rule. To learn more about that, check out my Credit Management 101 online course.

Remember, you are your only student loan debt advocate. Think of yourself that way!

CHAPTER 7 - UNDERSTANDING INTEREST

Compound/capitalization of interest. Capitalization of interest means the accrued interest is added to your principal amount and becomes a part of your principal balance so when interest is charged again, it will be charged on your original balance amount AND the interest that was added on to that amount. With federal loans, interest is capitalized at certain times during the life of your loan. (Incidentally, this is also how compounding works). For this section, let's begin with a list from an article on nerdwallet.com about the capitalization of unpaid interest reprinted below:

For federal student loans, capitalization of unpaid interest occurs:

- When the grace period ends on an unsubsidized loan.
- After a period of forbearance.
- After a period of deferment, for unsubsidized loans.
- If you leave the Revised Pay as You Earn (REPAYE), Pay as You Earn (PAYE) or Income-Based-Repayment (IBR) plan.
- If you don't recertify your income annually for the REPAYE, PAYE and IBR plans.
- If you no longer qualify to make payments based on your income under PAYE or IBR.
- If you're on the Income-Contingent Repayment (ICR) plan, it capitalizes annually.
- When you consolidate federal loans.

https://www.nerdwallet.com/article/loans/student-loans/student-loan-interest-capitalization

How your Income Driven Repayment plan treats interest. (THIS SECTION DOES NOT INCLUDE A DISCUSSION ON INTEREST FOR A 10 YEAR STANDARD REPAYMENT PLAN).

1. PAYE - payment MAY be less than the amount of interest accrued on the loan between monthly payments.

   For unsubsidized, eligible loans, if the payments are less than the accrued interest, it will be capitalized until the outstanding principal is 10% greater than the original principal amount. After that, interest will continue to accrue but will not be capitalized as long as the borrower remains in this plan.

   For subsidized, eligible loans, IF THE MONTHLY PAYMENT IS NOT ENOUGH TO PAY THE ACCRUED INTEREST, the Borrower is not charged the unpaid, accrued interest for three years (the three year period can be offset by any period of unpaid interest, i.e. in different plans, except for hardship deferment). Accrued interest is capitalized when Borrower no longer has a partial financial hardship or if they leave PAYE plan.

2. ICR - Payment MAY be less than the amount of interest accrued on the loan between monthly payments.

   After periods where a Borrower makes payment that is less than the interest accrued on the loan, the payment amount is recalculated based upon UNPAID ACCRUED INTEREST and the highest outstanding principal loan amount (INCLUDING AMOUNT CAPITALIZED) calculated for that Borrower while paying under the ICR plan. If Borrower's payment amount is less than accrued interest, unpaid interest is capitalized until the outstanding principal amount (original amount when loan entered repayment), is 10% greater than the original principal amount. After that, interest continues to accrue but is not capitalized.

3. 3. REPAYE - payment MAY be less than the amount of interest accrued on the loan between monthly payments. For Direct Unsubsidized, Direct PLUS made to a graduate or professional student, the unsubsidized portion of a Direct Consolidation Loan, or for a Direct Subsidized loan or the subsidized portion of a Direct Consolidation loan for which the Borrower has become responsible for accruing interest

because he/she is no longer eligible for subsidization, DOE charges 50% of the remaining accrued interest.

For subsidized, eligible loans, IF THE MONTHLY PAYMENT IS NOT ENOUGH TO PAY THE ACCRUED INTEREST, the Borrower is not charged the unpaid, accrued interest for three years. The three year period does not include any period of economic hardship. It includes any prior period of IBR or PAYE payments AND for Direct Consolidation Loans, any period in which the underlying loans under IBR or PAYE plans. Following this three year period, the DOE charges the Borrower 50% of the remaining accrued interest on the Direct Subsidized loan or the subsidized portion of a Direct Consolidation loan.

4. IBR - Payment MAY be less than the amount of interest accrued on the loan between monthly payments. For subsidized, eligible loans, IF THE MONTHLY PAYMENT IS NOT ENOUGH TO PAY THE ACCRUED INTEREST, the Borrower is not charged the remaining accrued interest for three years, (the three year period can be offset by any period of unpaid interest in PAYE or REPAYE. On Direct Consolidation (loans that repay loans on which the DOE has not charged Borrower accrued interest), the three year period includes the period for which the DOE did not charge the Borrower accrued interest on the underlying loans.) Periods of economic hardship deferment are not counted towards three year period. Accrued interest is capitalized when Borrower no longer has a partial financial hardship or if they leave IBR plan.

   - Amortization (negative amortization). Student loans are amortized loans. This means you borrow an amount one time and you pay it back via a fixed payment for a set period of time. The first payments start out going to interest and over time, shift to paying off the principal. If your student loan is not enough to pay off the interest, it will still accrue. This is called negative amortization and should be avoided if at all possible. Not likely if you are in an IDR plan. In that circumstance you could lose the benefit of the plan if your income becomes too high to qualify for a reduced payment.

5. Remember, the way interest accrues changes for each IDR plan is complicated. The reason I have included this information is to make you aware of how the actions you take can impact the accrual and/or capitalization of interest on your student loans. DO NOT take any action on your student loan debt without contacting your servicer and making sure you understand fully how your interest will be impacted.

Payment Scenarios:

In order to help you understand how interest accrues on different payment plans, there are 3 different scenarios for student borrowers and parent borrowers of dependent students below. The numbers in these scenarios are designed to be approximate (or estimates), just to give you an idea of how student loans operate. Finally, we are only using one Income Driven Repayment Plan scenario for the sake of efficiency, even though there are essentially four IDR plans. This is only intended to give you an idea of how interest accrues in an IDR plan.

Remember, ideally your monthly payments will be enough to cover accrued interest so there should be no interest to capitalize. However, capitalization on interest begins after you graduate if you haven't made any payments on it during the 4 years you are in school.

The correct way to calculate interest that accrues during school is to do it daily and break it down by each loan you acquire every semester (you wouldn't have 4 subsidized loans until you graduate), remembering that interest rates change annually (each year, the interest rates will likely be different).

What follows below is an estimated example of how interest accumulates in different scenarios, including while you are still in school. For the sake of convenience, we are calculating interest based on how much interest would accrue on the full amount after the borrower has at graduation using one interest rate for the entire 4 year period, as follows:

4 subsidized loans totaling $9,000 @ 4.53%

5 unsubsidized loans totaling $11,000 @ 4.53%

Interest accrued during school on unsubsidized loans - (assuming 4.53% for 8 semesters) = 1993.20 (all accrued interest will be capitalized at the end of your 6 month grace period).

Daily interest amount $1.24

At graduation, the total amount the graduate would owe in this scenario is $21,993.20.

<u>The 10 year standard repayment plan scenario for these numbers:</u>

You will be automatically defaulted into the 10 year standard repayment plan. This plan does not take your income into account. You will not be enrolled in an IDR unless you apply for one.

Monthly payment = $228.25

Total amount paid over 10 year repayment plan (including interest): $27,390.34

<u>Forbearance scenario:</u>

Lasts for 1 year and interest accumulates on subsidized and unsubsidized loans during that time period. If the borrower goes into forbearance immediately after graduating and only stays in forbearance for 1 year:

Interest accrued on $21,993.20 for 12 months = $996 (capitalized immediately after forbearance period ends)

Total amount owed = $22,989 Monthly payment goes up to: $239

<u>IDR payment scenario:</u>

Income Driven Repayment plans are designed to use your income to calculate a payment you can afford.

Assume your household AGI of $46,000 a year with a household size of 2 and income growth of 3.5% per year. Remember, you have to re-certify your income and household size every year. Your payment will change if your income goes up or your household size changes (for example, single parent whose child is no longer a live-in dependent after high school). In the PAYE plan, your payment/forgiveness scenario is as follows:

First monthly payment = $180 - Last month payment = $0 (your payment will change as your income and household size changes over the years, for this scenario your household size stays at 2).

Amount paid over 250 years (maximum repayment period): $28,249 (if your income does not change) Total amount of loan forgiven = $0

If your calculated payment is not enough to pay the interest that accumulates every month:

For unsubsidized, eligible loans, if the payments are less than the accrued interest, it will be capitalized until the outstanding principal is 10% greater than the original principal amount. **After that, interest will continue to accrue but will not be capitalized as long as the borrower remains in this plan.**

For subsidized, eligible loans, IF THE MONTHLY PAYMENT IS NOT ENOUGH TO PAY THE ACCRUED INTEREST, the Borrower is not charged the unpaid, accrued interest for 3 years (3 year period can be offset by any period of unpaid interest i.e. in different plans, except for hardship deferment. **Accrued interest is capitalized when Borrower no longer has a partial financial hardship or if they leave PAYE plan.**

---

2 Parent PLUS loans $15,000 @ 7.08%

PLUS loans come into repayment 60 days after they are disbursed. They also begin accruing interest immediately when disbursed. You must qualify for a PLUS loan meaning, you cannot have adverse credit.

daily interest rate = $2.85

The 10 year standard repayment plan scenario for these numbers:

Monthly payment = $174.78

Total interest paid = $5,973.92

Total amount paid over 10 year repayment plan: $20,973.92

Forbearance scenario:

Lasts for 1 year and interest accumulates on parent PLUS loans during that time period. If the borrower goes into forbearance immediately after the loan comes into repayment and only stays in forbearance for 1 year:

Interest accrued on $15,000.00 for 12 months = $1,062 (capitalized immediately after forbearance period ends)

Total amount owed = $16,062 Monthly payment goes up to: $187

ICR payment scenario:

This is the only income driven repayment plan available for parent PLUS loans.

AGI of $60,000 a year with a household size of 4 and income growth of 3.5% per year. In the ICR plan, your payment/forgiveness scenario is as follows:

First monthly payment = $155 - Last month payment = $157 (your payment will change as your income and household size changes over the years, for this scenario your household size stays at 4). Your payment will never be more than the 10 year standard payment amount.

Amount paid over 25 years (maximum repayment period): $22,301
Total amount of loan forgiven = $0

Payment MAY be less that the amount of interest accrued on the loan between monthly payments. After periods where a Borrower makes payment that is less than the interest accrued on the loan, the payment amount is recalculated based upon UNPAID ACCRUED

INTEREST & the highest outstanding principal loan amount (INCLUDING AMOUNT CAPITALIZED) calculated for that Borrower while paying under the ICR plan. If Borrower's payment amount is less than accrued interest, unpaid interest is capitalized until the outstanding principal amount (original amount when loan entered repayment), is 10% greater than the original principal amount. After that, interest continues to accrue but is not capitalized.

CHAPTER 8 - SERVICER HANDBOOK

- Remember that YOU and YOU ALONE are responsible for making sure your student loans are paid and the payments are applied correctly. The servicers are not your advocates. YOU are your student loan debt advocate. If you plan to "set it and forget it," you will likely be making a costly mistake.

- Your student loans are debts that you signed a contract for, meaning you agreed to pay them back when you signed on the dotted line. This means that you are responsible for paying them back even if your servicer is acting inappropriately, is subject to a lawsuit, or has turned your account over to collections.

- Do not fall victim to student loan debt attrition. Understand that you will need to check your student loan accounts on a routine basis, at least twice a month. You must be very watchful to make sure that each payment is applied and applied correctly. Check before you make a payment and after the payment clears, to make sure it was applied correctly.

- Documentation is your key to successfully paying off your student loans, student loan forgiveness, or even discharge. Do not be sloppy with documentation. Follow the steps for documenting your student loan information diligently. Do not get caught in the trap of not being able to prove a payment when you need to.

- Do not rely on your servicer to keep accurate records of your account.

- You could have multiple servicers if you have multiple student loans. Your servicers could change if your loans are transferred from one to another. Changing servicers should not change your interest rates. Your interest rates are set by the terms of your promissory note (the loan contract you signed with the Department of Education).

- Keep your contact information updated with your servicer. Your need to know information, like if your loan is being transferred, as soon as possible. Again, it is your responsibility to make sure your loan payment is being made every month, even if your loan changed servicers.

- Do not wait until the last minute to contact your servicer about a problem with your loan. The sooner you get ahead of a problem the better outcome you will have once it's resolved and the easier it will be to resolve it.

- Make sure you are prepared to call or email your servicer. Have all the information you need at hand like your payment and contact logs, cancelled checks, bank statements showing where payments cleared, etc.

- Remember, when you are on the phone with your servicer, be polite. Keep your emotions in check and ask to "speak to their supervisor" if you aren't getting information you need. Don't be afraid to state your issue, and ask for the information you are looking for.

- Don't forget to ask for a time frame for a response. You are perfectly within your rights to ask for a reply in a reasonable time frame.

- You could get different information based on how you contact your servicer. A standardized written response to an email may be more thorough for certain questions than a phone call to a customer service representative.

- While servicers are supposed to notify you of recertification deadlines, they may not. Ask what the deadline is for your recertification and put one or two reminders in your calendar that will give you plenty of time to complete your recertification paperwork (you'll do this online at: https://studentloans.gov/myDirectLoan/ibrInstructions.action not through your servicer).

- Try to avoid forbearance if you can. Servicers have been notorious in advising Borrowers to request forbearance rather than advising them about other repayment options.

- There is no penalty for early repayment but make sure your servicer is applying your additional payments correctly! Servicers will take your payment and apply it according to the payment priority guidelines in the Code of Federal Regulations (where the federal student loan debt regulations are). That means if you are paying extra on your loans every month, your payment will be "advanced" and the additional amount will be applied to next month's interest UNLESS you indicate otherwise. You have to SPECIFICALLY request that your servicer apply your additional payment to your principal. Contact your servicer to find out how to do this. It may mean simply checking a box somewhere on their website. Remember, each servicer is different so make sure you get confirmation from your servicer about this. You'll need to verify this for each servicer you have.

<u>Step 1 - Get Organized!</u>

1. Find out who your servicers are. You can start by checking the National Student Loan Data System: https://nslds.ed.gov/nslds/nslds_SA/

   You will need to login to the website (if you already have an FSA ID, which you should, it should work for this website).

2. Compare this information with the information on the studentaid.ed.gov (FSA) website to make sure everything looks the same (the websites should overlap).

3. If you feel like you are missing something, check your credit reports. In fact, you should be checking your credit reports regularly anyway. You are entitled to one free credit report per year from each of the nationwide credit reporting agencies, Equifax, Experian, and Transunion. You should not be required to enter a credit card to get your free credit report. Run one from each of the three agencies and compare them against the information from the

NSLDS/FSA website to make sure you have captured all your student loan debt accounts and information.

4. Familiarize yourself with your servicer's website. They will likely require you to use their website for all transactions regarding the loans they are servicing for you. You will probably need to create an account, username and password. Keep this information in a safe place and don't misplace it.

5. Make your payments on time! If your payment is not set on auto-pay (and there are pros and cons to this), set a reminder in your calendar on your smart phone to ensure you do not miss your payment. If your payment is even a day late, you can be considered delinquent.

Auto-Pay Pros:

- Convenience;
- Avoids late payments/delinquencies;
- May reduce your interest rate (usually less than 1%).

Auto-Pay Cons

- May overdraft your account if you aren't paying attention or you are in an IDR and fail to recertify;
- If you are in an IDR and you fail to recertify, your payment will go up automatically and your account will be charged the new, higher payment automatically, whether you are ready for it or not.

<u>Step 2 - Document, document, document!!</u>

1. Keep copies of every document you sign or get from your lender (DOE) and servicer. You should also have a copy of your promissory note and the terms and conditions of your account(s), make sure you read them carefully.

2. Begin by filling out the spreadsheet that you can download from newcashview.com/student-loans for free, don't forget

to read the spreadsheet instructions first! If you are more comfortable with hard copies, download/print the student loan information form instead. Print as many copies as you need to make sure you document each one of your student loans. Hole punch them and put them in a binder to ensure you don't lose them.

3. Every time you make a payment, log it into your spreadsheet on the "Payment Log" tab or on the downloadable payment log sheet. Do not skip this step! You MUST keep track of your payments. Again, you can print off the downloadable Payment Log form to track your payments. Print as many copies as you need to make sure you document each one of your student loans. Hole punch them and put them in a binder to ensure you don't lose them.

4. Keep proof of payment on the account. That means if you pay online, keep a screenshot of the receipt page with your confirmation number and make sure you can see the date, amount paid, and the account you are paying it out of.

   If you are old school and still write a check, get and keep your copies of the cancelled checks. Put all your copies in a safe place to make sure you don't lose them. They could make the difference between you paying what you owe or thousands of dollars more, if you have problems with your servicer maintaining your account accuracy. Screenshots are wonderful tools for online transactions. Make sure you are taking screenshots of everything you are submitting online.

   Also, verify the date the payment cleared your bank (especially if you do not pay by check). You can keep track of this in your Payment Log. It may seem like overkill, but as sure as night follows day, the minute you don't keep your own paper trail, you'll find yourself needing it to hold the servicer accountable.

5. Keep track of your communication with your servicer. Log each telephone conversation, letter, or item of paper correspondence, online chat, online contact (including email, filling out a "contact us" form on the servicer's, or any other

website, involving your student loans). Take note of what was discussed and what you agreed to (you and the servicer). You should log this into your spreadsheet on the "Contact Log" or "Correspondence Log" tabs (they are separated on the spreadsheet but combined on the downloadable form). You can print off the downloadable Student Loan Contact/Correspondence Log and use that if you are more comfortable with hard copies. Print as many copies as you need to make sure you document each one of your student loans. Hole punch them and put them in a binder to ensure you don't lose them.

This creates a paper trail that you will need if you have to resolve a problem with your servicer or lender at any point during the term of your loan. THIS INCLUDES YOUR RECERTIFICATION DOCUMENTATION! Again, take a screenshot of everything you submit online just to be sure you have the documentation you need should you have a problem in the future.

6. Follow the original document rule! This means you never send original documents to a servicer (or a lender, if you can help it), unless you have no other choice. Only send copies and your best bet is to send them certified mail, return receipt requested. That is the most surefire way to verify receipt. While this can be tedious (finding out your servicer's mailing address) and expensive it's at least $6.00 to send a certified letter, return receipt requested), it's the best way to ensure receipt.

   It's always best to communicate in writing, but sometimes it isn't possible. Do your very best to document each transaction and communication with your servicer. It will pay off when the time comes to make your last payment or for forgiveness on the remainder of your loan.

   Make sure you ask for confirmation of terms/outcome in writing. Have the servicer email or fax written verification of the outcome to you. Don't ever just "take their word for it," that they will do what you agreed upon. Remember, YOU are your own student loan debt advocate. Verify, verify, verify.

7. Ask for your payment history. It is a good idea to ask for your payment history periodically and compare it to your own payment records. This is especially true if you have noticed a discrepancy between your records and your servicer account.

<u>Step 3 - Verify, verify, verify!</u>

1. Review your account balance carefully. It is not uncommon for mistakes in payment amounts or application so keep a close eye on your account balance. You should know what your principal payment is, your interest payment (including how interest is being treated in your repayment plan), and any fees you've been charged (like collection or late fees).

2. Check back to make sure the servicer did what they were supposed to do. Did they enroll you into the repayment plan per your request? Did they apply the payment as you requested? Did they correct the mistake in your account/payment history? Did they change the mailing address on your account? You have to double check and make sure they are doing what they said they would do.

Managing your student loan debt is just the first step in getting your personal finances under control and building wealth. Student loans are also just a part of understanding how to manage your credit. A great starting point for both managing your credit and starting to build wealth is learning how to budget. You can do all of these things by heading over to newcashview.com and enrolling in our 60 Minute Budget Bootcamp and our Credit Management 101 online course. These courses are designed to help you learn the techniques you need to manage every aspect of your credit and get started with a budget.

Thank you for purchasing this guide. I hope it serves you well and puts you on the path to financial freedom!

ABOUT THE AUTHOR

Joy Alford-Brand is an attorney, author, public speaker and personal finance educator. After more than a decade in bankruptcy practice, she decided to start newcashview.com as a platform to teach people smart and simple money management techniques to help them live happier, more peaceful lives. You can find her content on the following platforms:

Instagram: @joyalfordbrand
YouTube: ncvtv
Facebook: facebook.com/newcashview
LinkedIn: linkedin.com/in/joyalfordbrand
Twitter: @ncvcom1
Pinterest: newcashview.com

Made in United States
Troutdale, OR
11/03/2026

56845101R00031